THE SEVEN LAMPS OF ADVOCACY

THE SEVEN LAMPS OF ADVOCACY

By

His Honour Judge **EDWARD ABBOTT PARRY**

GYAN

Published by

GYAN

Gyan Publishing House
5, Ansari Road
Daryaganj, New Delhi-110002
Phone: 011-47034999, 9811692060
E-mail: books@gyanbooks.com

Distribution Network
gyanbooks.com
India, USA, Canada, UK, Australia

ISBN: 978-93-6208-555-9 (HB)
First Published, 1923

2nd Impression 2024

Printed at: Gyan Press, Delhi.

THE SEVEN LAMPS OF ADVOCACY
Author: EDWARD ABBOTT PARRY

THE SEVEN LAMPS OF ADVOCACY

THE SEVEN LAMPS OF ADVOCACY

By *His Honour Judge* EDWARD ABBOTT PARRY

T. FISHER UNWIN LTD
LONDON: ADELPHI TERRACE

TO

THE NORTHERN CIRCUIT

WHERE I LEARNED

THESE THINGS

CONTENTS

I

THE LAMP OF HONESTY

I

THE LAMP OF HONESTY

THE great advocate is like the great actor: he fills the stage for his span of life, succeeds, gains our applause, makes his last bow, and the curtain falls. Nothing is so elusive as the art of acting, unless indeed it be the sister art of advocacy. You cannot say that the methods of Garrick, Kean or Irving, Erskine, Hawkins or Russell, were the right methods or the only methods, or even that they were the best methods of practising their several arts; you can only say that they succeeded in their day, and that their contemporaries acclaimed them as masters.

Inasmuch as their methods were often new and startling to their own generation, the young student of acting or advocacy is eager to believe that there are no methods and no technique to learn, and no school in which to graduate. Youth is at all times prone to act on the principle that there are no principles, that there is no one from whom it can learn, and nothing to teach. Any one, it seems, can don a wig and gown, and thereby become an advocate. Yet there are principles of advocacy; and if a few generations were to forget to practise these, it would indeed be a lost art. The student of advocacy can draw inspiration and hope from the stored-up experience of his elders. He can trace in the plans and life-charts of the ancients the paths along which they strode, journeying towards Eldorado. True, these figures of forgotten advocates are dim and obscure—only to be painfully seen through the dusty gauzes of forgotten years, pictured for us in drowsy voluminous memoirs, or baldly reported in mouldering law reports; but if we search these records diligently we gradually discern a race of worthy men—see them haunting the old libraries, pacing the ancient halls with their clients, proud of the traditions of their great profession—advocates—advocates all.

It is in an endeavour to recapture something of the lives of these great ones, and the principles upon which they built their success, that I have struggled through forbidding masses of decaying biography in hopes to catch a faint whisper here and there of the triumphant works and days of my professional forbears.

For a race of moderns, that, maybe, care for none of these things, I have lighted again the old lamps which burned so brightly in the days that are gone, which I myself have seen lighting the darkness of our courts, and guiding the footsteps of the judges in the paths of justice and truth. For without a free and honourable race of advocates the world will hear little of the message of justice. Advocacy is the outward and visible appeal for the spiritual gift of justice. The advocate is the priest in the temple of justice, trained in the mysteries of the creed, active in its exercises. For this reason Wyclif in his translation of I John ii. 1 sanctifies the word in the text: "We haue auoket anentis the fadir, Jhesu Crist just." Modern versions retain "advocate," but unhappily substitute "righteous" for "just." Advocacy connotes justice. Upon the altars of justice the advocate must keep his seven lamps clean and burning brightly. In the centre of these must ever be the lamp of honesty.

The English Bar is a society of advocates, though, as Blackstone tells us, we generally call them counsel. The Scots retain the name in their Faculty of Advocates The word must be insisted upon for its ancientry and meaning. The order of advocates is, in D'Aguesseau's famous phrase, "as noble as virtue." Far back in the Capitularies of Charlemagne it was ordained of the profession of advocates "that nobody should be admitted therein but men mild, pacific, fearing God, and loving justice, upon pain of elimination." So may it continue, world without end.

From the earliest, Englishmen have understood that advocacy is necessary to justice, and honesty is essential to advocacy. The thirteenth century *Mirrour of Justices* may, as modern jurists hold, be a contemptible legal compilation. It is said to have been written by one Andrew Horn, a fishmonger; and what could he have known, say the learned ones, about the origin and history of legal affairs? Nevertheless, to the reader of to-day the views of the man in the street, the common citizen of a bygone age, about the place in the world of the advocate is more precious than many black-letter folios of crabbed juridical learning.

"Some there be," says our fishmonger very shrewdly, "who know not how to state their causes or to defend them in court, and some who cannot, and therefore are pleaders necessary; so that what plaintiffs and others cannot or know not how to do by themselves they may do by their serjeants, proctors, or friends. Pleaders are serjeants wise in the law of the realm who serve the commonality of the people, stating and defending for hire actions in court for those who have need of them. Every pleader who acts in the business of another should have regard to four things:—First, that he be a person receivable in court, that he be no heretic, nor excommunicate, nor criminal, nor man of religion, nor woman, nor ordained clerk above the order of sub-deacon, nor beneficed clerk with the cure of souls, nor infant under twenty-one years of age, nor judge in the same cause, nor open leper, nor man attainted of falsification against the law of his office. Secondly, that every pleader is bound by oath that he will not knowingly maintain or defend wrong or falsehood, but will abandon his client immediately that he perceives his wrong-doing. Thirdly, that he will never have recourse to false delays or false witnesses, and never allege, proffer, or consent to any corruption, deceit, lie, or falsified law, but loyally will maintain the right of his client, so that he may not fail through his folly or negligence, nor by default of him, nor by default of any argument that he could urge; and that he will not by blow, contumely, brawl, threat, noise, or villain conduct disturb any judge, party, serjeant, or other in court, nor impede the hearing or the course of justice. Fourthly, there is the salary, concerning which four points must be regarded—the amount of the matter in dispute, the labour of the serjeant, his value as a pleader in respect of his (learning), eloquence, and repute, and lastly the usage of the court."

Note how from the earliest days the advocate may in no way maintain or defend wrong or falsehood. It is the right of his client he is there to uphold, and the right only. Nevertheless, although an advocate is bound by obligations of honour and probity not to overstate the truth of his client's case, and is forbidden to have recourse to any artifice or subterfuge which may beguile the judge, he is not the judge of the case, and within these limits must use all the knowledge and gifts he possesses to advance his client's claims to justice.

Many good men have been troubled with the thought that advocacy implied a certain want of honesty. Boswell asked Doctor Johnson whether he did not think "that the practice of the law in some degree hurt the nice feeling of honesty?"

To whom the doctor replied: "Why no, Sir, if you act properly. You are not to deceive your clients with false representations of your opinion: you are not to tell lies to a judge." *Boswell:* "But what do you think of supporting a cause which you know to be bad?" *Johnson:* "Sir, you do not know it to be good or bad till the judge determines it. I have said that you are to state facts fairly; so that your thinking, or what you call knowing, a cause to be bad must be from reasoning, must be from your supposing your arguments to be weak and inconclusive. But, Sir, that is not enough. An argument which does not convince yourself, may convince the judge to whom you urge it: and if it does convince him, why, then, Sir, you are wrong, and he is right. It is his business to judge; and you are not to be confident in your own opinion that a cause is bad, but to say all you can for your client, and then hear the Judge's opinion." *Boswell:* "But, Sir, does not affecting a warmth when you have no warmth, and appearing to be clearly of one opinion when you are in reality of another opinion, does not such dissimulation impair one's honesty? Is there not some danger that a lawyer may put on the same mask in common life, in the intercourse with his friends ?" *Johnson:* "Why no, Sir, everybody knows you are paid for affecting warmth for your client; and it is, therefore, properly no dissimulation: the moment you come from the bar you resume your usual behaviour. Sir, a man will no more carry the artifice of the bar into the common intercourse of society, than a man who is paid for tumbling upon his hands will continue to tumble upon his hands when he should walk on his feet."

I like the rough English common-sense of this; but the Irishman in the dock had an inspired vision of the same truth when, in answer to the Clerk of the Crown, who called upon him with the familiar interrogatory, "Guilty or Not Guilty?" he replied with a winning smile, "And how can I tell till I hear the evidence?"

When Lord Brougham, at a dinner to M. Berryer, claimed in his speech that the advocate should reckon everything as subordinate to the interests of his client, Lord Chief Justice Cockburn, "feeling that our guest might leave us with a false impression of our ideals," set forth his views of an advocate's duty, concluding with these memorable words: "The arms which an advocate wields he ought to use as a warrior, not as an assassin. He ought to uphold the interests of his client *per fas*, and not *per nefas*. He ought to know how to reconcile the interests of his clients with the eternal interests of truth and justice."

The best advocates of all generations have been devotees of honesty. Abraham Lincoln founded his fame and success in the profession on what some called his "perverse honesty." On his first appearance in the Supreme Court of Illinois he addressed the court as follows: "This is the first case I have ever had in this court, and I have therefore examined it with great care. As the court will perceive by looking at the abstract of the record, the only question in the case is one of authority. I have not been able to find any authority to sustain my side of the case, but I have found several cases directly in point on the other side. I will now give these authorities to the court, and then submit the case."

There have been advocates who regard such a course as quixotic. The late Joshua Williams was asked whether, if an advocate knows of a decided case in point against him which he has reason to believe is not known to the other side, he is bound to reveal it, and gave it as his opinion that "in principle this is no part of his duty as an advocate." It must be remembered that this opinion was given when a host of cases were decided against their merits on purely technical points of law; but there is no doubt what the practice ought to be, and what among English advocates the practice is.

If an advocate knows the law to be *x*, it is not honest to lead the court to believe that it is *y*. Whether the advocate does this by directly mis-stating the law, or by deliberately omitting to state it fully within the means of his knowledge, it is equally without excuse, and dims the lamp of honesty.

For the advocate must remember that he is not only the servant of the client, but the friend of the court, and honesty is as essential to true friendship as it is to sound advocacy.

II

THE LAMP OF COURAGE

II

THE LAMP OF COURAGE

ADVOCACY needs the "king-becoming graces: devotion, patience, courage, fortitude." Advocacy is a form of combat where courage in danger is half the battle. Courage is as good a weapon in the forum as in the camp. The advocate, like Cæsar, must stand upon his mound facing the enemy, worthy to be feared, and fearing no man.

Unless a man has the spirit to encounter difficulties with firmness and pluck, he had best leave advocacy alone. Richard Bethell, Lord Westbury, in early life took for his motto: "*De l'audace et encore de l'audace, et toujours de l'audace.*" In advising on a case he was always clear and direct, saying that he was "paid for his opinion, not for his doubts." Charles Hatton, writing as a layman of Jeffreys in his early days at the bar, shrewdly notes his best quality: "He hath in perfection the three chief qualifications of a lawyer: Boldness, Boldness, Boldness." A modern advocate kindly reproving a junior for his timidity of manner wisely said: " Remember it is better to be strong and wrong than weak and right."

The belief that success in advocacy can be attained by influence, apart from personal qualifications, is ill-founded. There was never a youngster with better backing than Francis North, afterwards Lord Keeper to Charles II., yet, as his biographer says, " observe his preparatives," his earnest attendances at moots, his diligent waiting in that " dismal hole " the " corner chamber, one pair of stairs in Elm Court."

In the same way his younger brother, Roger, though born in the ermine, so to speak, had to plod his way up like any other junior. It is good tc be the brother of a Lord Chancellor, but it does not make a man an advocate.

Roger North's autobiography is full of interest to the student of advocacy. His memory of his first appearance is vivid and entertaining. " I was immediately called," he writes, " to the Bar, *ex gratiâ*, not having standing, although I had performed such exercises as the house required, save a few. My first flight in practice was the opening a declaration at *Nisi Prius* in Guildhall, under my brother, which was a crisis like the loss of a maidenhead; but with blushing and blundering I got through it, and afterwards grew bold and ready at such a formal performance; but it was long ere I adventured to ask a witness a question."

Roger North would never have attained the eminence he did in his profession by merely hanging on to the gown of his greater brother. Hard work and dogged courage, not patronage, earned him the dignities he achieved. The description of his early beginnings is full of encouragement for the young advocate. "During my practice under Hale," he says, "at the King's Bench I was raw, and not at all quaint and forward as some are, so that I did but learn experience and discover my own defects, which were very great. I was a plant of a slow growth, and when mature but slight wood, and of a flashy fruit. But my profession obliged me to go on, which I resolved to do against all my private discouragements, and whatever absurdities and errors I committed in public I would not desist, but forgot them as fast as I could, and took more care another time. My comfort was, if some, all did not see my failings, and those upon whom I depended, the attorneys and suitors, might think the pert and confident forwardness I put on might produce somewhat of use to them."

North held the sound opinion that "he who is not a good lawyer before he comes to the Bar, will never be a good one after it." It is very true that learning begets courage, and wise self-confidence can only be founded on knowledge. The long years of apprenticeship, the studious attention to "preparatives," are, to the advocate, like the manly exercises of the young squire that enabled the knight of old to earn his spurs on the field of battle. In no profession is it more certain that "knowledge is power," and when the opportunity arrives, knowledge, and the courage to use it effectively, proclaim the presence of the advocate.

The best instance of what is meant perhaps may be found in Sir John Hollams's account of the first appearance of Mr. Benjamin. He was a great lawyer before he addressed the court, but he sat down a great advocate. It was in a case which came on for hearing before Lord Justice James, then Vice-Chancellor, and "it appeared to be generally thought that, as usual at the time, a decree would be made directing inquiries in chambers. The matter was being so dealt with when Mr. Benjamin, then unknown to any one in Court, rose from the back seat in the Court. He had not a commanding presence, and at that time had rather an uncouth appearance. He, in a stentorian voice, not in accord with the quiet tone usually prevailing in the Court of Chancery, startled the Court by saying, 'Sir, notwithstanding the somewhat off-hand and supercilious manner in which this case has been dealt with by my learned friend Sir Roundell Palmer, and to some extent acquiesced in by my learned leader Mr. Kay, if, sir, you will only listen to me—if, sir, you will only listen to me' (repeating the same words three times, and on each occasion raising his voice), 'I pledge myself you will dismiss this suit with costs.' The Vice-Chancellor and Sir Roundell Palmer, and indeed all the Court, looked at him with a kind of astonishment, but he went on without drawing rein for between two and three hours. The Court became crowded, for it soon became known that there was a very unusual scene going on. In the end the Vice-Chancellor did dismiss the suit with costs, and his decision was confirmed on appeal."

There have been many advocates whose courage was founded on humour rather than knowledge, and who have successfully asserted their independence in the face of an impatient or overbearing Bench through the medium of wit, where mere wisdom might have failed in effect.

Of such was Tom Jones, who startled Mr. Justice Byles into indignant attention by opening his case with bold impertinence: "No one, my lords, who looks at this case with common fairness and honesty, can hesitate for a moment in declaring that there ought to be a new trial."

Byles observed, "This is rather strong language to use to us, Mr. Jones. I hope you think that we, at the least, are commonly fair and honest."

"We shall see, my lord," said Tom; "we shall see."

Serjeant Robinson tells us a further good story of Tom's refusal to be hustled by the Bench.

"Our friend Tom Jones," he writes, "was a little lengthy sometimes in the exposition of his client's rights, and one day the chief baron said to him, 'Mr. Jones, this case has occupied a great deal of time, and we have a very long list of cases to get through.'

"'My lord,' said Tom, 'I have carefully looked through that list, and I did not find there was a single cause in which I or my client was in the slightest degree interested.' "

But these sallies should never degenerate into mere incivility or abuse, in which there is little real courage, since a judge of sense will always refrain, if it be at all possible, from reply to such attacks, which only injure the reputation of the Bar and destroy the reputation of the advocate.

In the early days of American Sessions a certain judge was violently attacked by a young and very impudent attorney. To the manifest surprise of everybody present, the judge heard him quite through as though unconscious of what was said, and made no reply. After the adjournment of the day, and all had assembled at the inn where the judge and many of the attorneys had their lodgings, one of the company, referring to the scene in court, asked the judge why he did not rebuke the impertinent fellow.

"Permit me," said the judge, loud enough to call the attention of all the company, among whom was the fellow in question—" permit me to tell you a story. My father, when we lived down in the country, had a dog—a mere puppy, I may say. Well, this puppy would go out every moonlight night and bark at the moon for hours together." Here the judge paused, as if he had done with his story.

"Well, what of it?" exclaimed half-a-dozen of the audience at once.

"Oh, nothing, nothing whatever; the moon kept right on, as if nothing had happened."

Independence without moderation becomes licentiousness, but true independence is an essential attribute of advocacy, and the English Bar has never wanted men endowed with this form of true courage. The sacrifice of the highest professional honours to the maintenance of principle has been a commonplace in the history of English advocates, and the names of the living could be added if need be to those who have passed away, leaving us this clean heritage as example.

The true position of the independence of the English Bar, the right and the duty of the advocate to appear in every case, however poor, degraded, or wicked the party may be, is laid down once and for all in a celebrated speech of Erskine's in his defence of Thomas Paine, who was indicted in 1792 for publishing the *Rights of Man*. Great public indignation was expressed against Erskine for daring to defend Paine. As he said in his speech, "In every place where business or pleasure collects the public together, day after day, my name and character have been the topics of injurious reflection. And for what? Only for not having shrunk from the discharge of a duty which no personal advantage recommended, and which a thousand difficulties repelled."

He then continued, in words which the learned editor of Howell's State Trials emphasises by printing in capital letters, to enunciate one of the basic principles of English advocacy:

"Little, indeed, did they know me, who thought that such calumnies would influence my conduct: I WILL FOR EVER, AT ALL HAZARDS, ASSERT THE DIGNITY, INDEPENDENCE, AND INTEGRITY OF THE ENGLISH BAR; WITHOUT WHICH, IMPARTIAL JUSTICE, THE MOST VALUABLE PART OF THE ENGLISH CONSTITUTION, CAN HAVE NO EXISTENCE. From the moment that any advocate can be permitted to say that he will or will not stand between the Crown and the subject arraigned in the court where he daily sits to practise—from that moment the liberties of England are at an end. If the advocate refuses to defend, from what he may think of the charge or of the defence, he assumes the character of the judge; nay, he assumes it before the hour of judgment; and, in proportion to his rank and reputation, puts the heavy influence of perhaps a mistaken opinion into the scale against the accused, in whose favour the benevolent principle of English law makes all presumptions, and which commands the very judge to be his counsel."

Side by side with this may be set the grand example of William Henry Seward in acting in the defence of the negro Freeman in 1846. A horrible murder was committed. Without any provocation or desire for plunder, Freeman killed a farmer and several of his family. He was easily captured, when he laughed in the face of his captors and acknowledged the crime. He was a recently emancipated slave, deaf, and obviously insane. The sheriff had the greatest difficulty in preventing him from being lynched. The clergyman at the victims' funeral made a rousing appeal for his punishment, which was printed and circulated round the district.

Seward undertook his defence, and a storm of prejudice and passion was directed against him to dissuade him from doing what he believed to be his duty as an advocate. In the crowded court-house, when the judge asked, "Will any one defend this man ?" and Seward rose, and said he was counsel for the prisoner, a murmur of indignation ran round the court. His advocacy was of no avail to the individual, but his eloquent speech remains a noble statement of the duty of the advocate, and a fine example of devotion and courage in the exercise of that duty.

The whole speech is worthy of study, as it contains a glowing and reasoned appeal for the right of the most degraded human being in a civilised state to a real hearing of his case in a judicial court, which can only be obtained through honest and competent advocacy.

As the yellow harvest-moon rose outside the darkening court-house his peroration was listened to by the indignant crowd with, at least, outward respect, and it remains a message of encouragement to the advocates of future generations.

"In due time, gentlemen of the jury, when I shall have paid the debt of nature, my remains will rest here in your midst with those of my kindred and neighbours. It is very possible they may be unhonoured, neglected, spurned! But perhaps years hence, when the passion and excitement which now agitate this community shall have passed away, some wandering stranger, some lone exile, some Indian, some negro, may erect over them an humble stone, and thereon this epitaph : 'He was faithful.' "

These words, as he desired, are engraved on the marble over him, and he is remembered at the American Bar as an advocate who upheld its best traditions, and feared not to hold aloft the Lamp of Courage.

III

THE LAMP OF INDUSTRY

III

THE LAMP OF INDUSTRY

THE first task of the advocate is to learn to labour and to wait. There never was a successful advocate who did not owe some of his prowess to industry. From the biographies of our ancestors we may learn that the eminent successful ones of each generation practised at least enough industry in their day to preach its virtues to aspiring juniors.

Work soon becomes a habit. It may not be altogether a good habit, but it is better to wear out than to rust out. Nothing, we are told, is impossible to industry. Certainly without industry the armoury of the advocate will lack weapons on the day of battle.

There must be years of what Charles Lamb described with graceful alliteration as "the dry drudgery of the desk's dead wood" before the young advocate can hope to dazzle juries with eloquent perorations, confound dishonest witnesses by skilful cross-examination, and lead the steps of erring judges into the paths of precedent.

All great advocates tell us that they have had either steady habits of industry or grand outbursts of work. Charles Russell had a continuous spate of energy. Many of us can remember him, tireless and active himself, bustling into the robing-room at St. George's Hall, Liverpool, and finding several members of the Junior Bar standing around the fire.

"Why are you loafing about here?" he asked. "Why don't you *do* something?"

"We have nothing to do," said the Junior Bar.

"Why don't you go to the races?" he rejoined. "*Do* something!"

Abraham Lincoln owed his sound knowledge of law to grim, zealous industry. As a storekeeper he studied Blackstone out of shop-hours, perched on a wood-pile or lying under a tree. On circuit, in the bedroom of the village inn, a candle at his head and his feet protruding over the foot-board of his bed, he lay reading law until two in the morning, undisturbed by snoring comrades. When possible, he would read aloud, for thus, he said, "two senses catch the idea. First, I see what I read; second, I hear it, and can therefore remember it better." In after-life to every student who came near him his advice was, "Work! work! work!"

Advocacy is indeed a life of industry. Each new success brings greater toil. Campbell, writing home from the Oxford Circuit, describes the weary round of his daily task. Some advocates suffer thus every day the court sits, whilst others sit round and suffer envy.

"I ought to have got so far to-night on my way to Hereford, but we have a long day's work before us, and I shall be obliged to travel all to-morrow night. You can hardly form a notion of the life of labour, anxiety, and privation which I lead upon the circuit. I am up every morning by six. I never get out of court till seven, eight, or nine in the evening, and, having swallowed any indifferent fare that my clerk provides for me at my lodgings, I have consultations and read briefs till I fall asleep. This arises very much from the incompetence of the judge. It is from the incompetency of judges that the chief annoyances I have in life arise. I could myself have disposed of the causes here in half the time the judge employed. He has tried two causes in four days. Poor fellow, he is completely knocked up."

An advocate must study his brief in the same way that an actor studies his part. Success in advocacy is not arrived at by intuition. Mr. O'Brien, in his excellent biography of Charles Russell, details an interesting conversation with his hero which enforces this truth. He had raised the question of an advocate succeeding by mere intuition in picking up the threads of a case in court, when Russell interrupted him in a characteristic phrase. "'That's all nonsense,' he said. 'You don't know anything by intuition. You have to work hard and to think hard. I get some good help, as I tell you. My mode of work is this: One of these young men reads the brief and makes a note—a full one. I go through the note with him' (smiling), 'cross-examining him, if you like. Sometimes, I admit, it may not be necessary for me to read the brief; the note may be so complete, and the man's knowledge of the case so exact, that I get everything from him. But it often is—in fact, generally is—necessary to go to the brief. You have seen me reading briefs here. I admit that I am quick in getting at the kernel of a case, and that saves me some trouble; but I must read the brief with my own eyes, or somebody else's.'

"I said, 'Sir John Karslake went blind because he could only read his brief with his own eyes. It is a great point to be able to read your brief with somebody else's eyes!'

"*Russell*—'Well, well, well, that's so! but it is not intuition.'

"I said, 'It has been said that O'Connell never read his brief when he appeared for the defendant. He made his case out of the plaintiff's case.'

"*Russell*—'I don't think that is likely; I think O'Connell knew his case—the vital points in his case—before he went into court. There is often a great deal in a brief which is not vital, which is not even pertinent. I can read a brief quickly; I can take in a page at a glance, if you like; I can throw the rubbish over easily, and come right on the marrow of the case. But I can only do that by reading the brief, or by the help of my friends. I learn a great deal at consultations; I am not above taking hints from everybody, and I think carefully over everything that is said to me' (holding his hand up with open palm); 'I shut out no view. If I have a good point, it is that I can see quickly the hinge on which the whole case turns, and I never lose sight of it. But that is not intuition, my friend; it is work.'"

Industry in reading and book-learning may make a man a good jurist, but the advocate must exercise his industry in the double art of speaking and arranging his thoughts in ordered speech. He must be ready to leave his books awhile and practise the athletics of eloquence with equal industry.

The silver-tongued Heneage Finch advises students "to study all the morning and talk all the afternoon." Old Serjeant Maynard, deeply learned in booklore as he was, described the calling of the advocate as *ars bablativa.* Brougham told the law students of London University to habituate themselves to talk about everything.

For "bare reading without practice pedantiseth a student, but never makes him a clever lawyer." Our fathers understood this better perhaps than we do, and made provision of halls and cloisters and gardens, where students could take exercise and discuss the mysteries of their profession when the hours of reading were over.

Roger North tells us in his life of his brother, the Lord Keeper: "I remember that, after the fire of the Temple, it was considered whether the old cloister walks should be rebuilt or rather improved into chambers; which latter had been for the benefit of the Middle Temple. But in regard it could not be done without the consent of the Inner house, the masters of the Middle house waited upon the then Mr. Attorney Finch, to desire the concurrence of his society upon a proposition of some benefit to be thrown in on that side. But Mr. Attorney would by no means give way to it, and reproved the Middle Templars very wittily and eloquently upon the subject of students walking in evenings there and putting cases, 'which,' he said, 'was done in his time, as mean and low as the buildings were then, however it comes that such a benefit to students is now made so little account of.' And thereupon the cloisters, by the order and disposition of Sir Christopher Wren, were built as they now stand."

The days of wandering in cloisters and gardens, putting cases to one's fellow-students, and listening to the wisdom of elders by the margin of the fountain are, alas! not for us. But even to-day a wise youngster should recognise that sitting in court to listen to the conduct of cases, attendance at circuit mess and dining in Hall, where the law-talk of seniors may still on occasion be of value—these things are all forms of industry, for the advocate can only learn the true creed of his faith from oral tradition.

In recent years we have wisely revived

the old moots which date back to early days when the Inns of Court were really schools of law. Dugdale thus describes the ancient ceremony of the moot: "The pleadings are first recited by the students, then the case heard and argued by the barristers; and lastly by the reader elect and benchers, who all three argue in English; but the pleadings are recited, and the case argued by the utter barristers, in law French. The moot being ended, all parties return to the cupboard, where the mootmen present the benchers with a cup of beer and a slice of bread."

Roger North also remembers that in his day, the time of Charles II., the custom of mooting had been discontinued for upwards of a century; but modern wisdom brings us back to many old customs of our fathers, and to-day all dramatic methods of education are recognised as of greater value than dictatorial lectures.

And not only are these more social forms of industry good in themselves, but they are the only antidote to that despondency and dread of failure which cloud the brightest and most hopeful mind in the long days of apprenticeship. Even the greatest advocates have suffered such moments. Had John Scott yielded to his own sinking inclinations, he might have been a provincial barrister at Newcastle instead of Lord Chancellor; Kenyon nearly became a Welsh parson instead of Chief Justice of England; and Russell tells us that in our own day Gully nearly exiled himself to the Straits Settlements, and Herschell proposed to emigrate to the Indian Bar.

A learned County Court judge, in dealing with the unfortunate bankruptcy of a brother-barrister, expressed the opinion that for a man to come to the Bar without private means, or, at least, expectations from a maiden aunt, was "a rash and hazardous speculation." His dictum was unsound in law and history. Some of the greatest advocates began life as poor men. And though men of wealth have succeeded in advocacy, yet poverty is a true friend to industry. "Parts and poverty," said Lord Chancellor Talbot, "are the only things needed by the law student."

Kenyon, when asked by a fashionable lady how her son might best prepare for success at the Bar, said: "Let him spend all his money, marry a rich wife, spend all hers, and when he has got not a shilling in the world, let him attack the law." For a lawyer, as an old pleader said, must be prepared in his early days "to eat sawdust without butter," or, as

Lord Eldon put it, "to live like a hermit and work like a horse."

If a man is endowed with health and industry, the profession of an advocate is not "a rash and hazardous speculation." He may even without blame give hostages to fortune, remembering that when Erskine made his first appearance at the Bar his agitation nearly overcame him, and he was just about to sit down a failure when, he says, "I thought I felt my little children tugging at my gown, and the idea roused me to an exertion of which I did not think myself capable." He succeeded, indeed, far beyond his expectations, and he found, when he had overcome that first modest inertia which benumbs even the greatest genius, that he was fully equipped to fight the battles of his clients against all comers. And the reason of it was that he had not failed to read and learn and digest beneath the Lamp of Industry.

IV

THE LAMP OF WIT

IV

THE LAMP OF WIT

At the back of this little word "wit" lies the idea of knowledge, understanding, sense. In its manifestation we look for a keen perception of some incongruity of the moment. The murky atmosphere of the court is illuminated by a flash of thought, quick, happy, and even amusing. Wit, wisely used, bridges over a difficulty, smooths away annoyance, or perhaps turns aside anger, dissolving embarrassment in a second's laughter.

Nor can "(laughter in court)," a derogatory parenthesis unknown in the official law reports, be wholly condemned among human men. "How much lies in laughter, the cipher key wherewith we decipher the whole man!" Laughter may be derisive, unkind, even cruel, or it may be rightly used as a just weapon of ridicule wherewith to smite pretension and humbug. It may be gracious and full of kindliness, putting a timid man at his ease, or instinct with good-humour, softening wrath or mitigating tedious irrelevancy. It may be the due recognition of a witty text preaching a useful truth, that could otherwise be expressed only in a treatise; as when Common Law said unto Chancery, "Truth will leak out even in an affidavit;" or when Erskine replied to Kenyon, who suggested that he should apply to Chancery for relief, "Would your lordship send a dog you loved there?"

From the earliest times wit has been a light to lighten the darkness of advocacy. Cicero was noted for the jests and repartees which punctuated his forensic speeches, and these were held "not foreign to the business of the forum." Yet, like many a man of wit, he stumbled on occasion through the temptation of the gift, and offended some with malevolent sayings, as Bethell and others have done in our own time. It is easy to forget the poet's warning about "the medium in all things."

Pedants and bores resent all forms of wit, but a real humorist rejoices in nothing so much as a good story against himself. Rufus Choate was a man of great eloquence and abounding vocabulary, but he had a true sense of wit. No one enjoyed better the remark of Mr. Justice Wilde, a dry, precise judge who, out of court, on occasion allowed his wit expression. He was asked by a junior if he had not heard that Mr. Worcester had just published a new edition of his dictionary with a great number of additional words. Gripping his young friend's arm, he said in a perturbed whisper, "No, I had not heard of it. But, for God's sake, don't tell Choate!"

Choate had his own wit, which charmed many juries to his clients' cause. No one could more pleasantly disperse the frowning morality of a common jury by a human simile. What could be more pastoral and poetical than his description of his clients in an Arcadian divorce case? "They were playful, gentlemen of the jury, not guilty. After the morning toil they sat down upon the hay-mow for refreshment, not crime. There may have been a little youthful fondling, playful, not amorous. They only wished to *soften the asperities of hay-making*." One can see the jury broadening into sympathy and smiles over the pleasantry of the final phrase.

Often the wit of an advocate will turn a judge from an unwise course where argument or rhetoric would certainly fail. Lord Mansfield paid little attention to religious holidays. He would sit on Ash-Wednesday, to the scandal of some members of the Bar, whose protests made no impression upon him. At the end of Lent he suggested that the court might sit on Good Friday. The members of the Bar were horrified. Serjeant Davy, who was in the case, bowed in acceptance of the proposition. "If your lordship pleases; but your lordship will be the first judge that has done so since Pontius Pilate." The court adjourned until Saturday.

But the learned Serjeant "Bull Davy," as he was called on circuit, could never pass a jest, even at the expense of his client. He was defending a criminal against whom the prosecution had opened a very strong case.

"Who is concerned for the prisoner?"

"My lord," replied Davy, rising with grave solemnity, "I am concerned for him, and very much concerned, after what I have heard."

Wit is often the fittest instrument with which to destroy the bubble of bombast. When Curran, in an outburst of histrionic anger, placed his hand upon his heart, saying, "I am the trusty guardian of my own honour," it was Sir Boyle Roche who spoiled the episode by rising with much friendliness to say, "I congratulate my honourable friend on the snug little sinecure to which he has appointed himself."

Wit may fairly be used to strip the cloak of pretension from the shoulders of impudence. Holker was cross-examining a big vulgar Jew jeweller in a money-lending case and began by looking him up and down in a sleepy dismal way and drawled out: "Well, Mr. Moselwein, and what are you?"

"A genschelman," replied the jeweller with emphasis.

"Just so, just so," ejaculated Holker with a dreary yawn, "but what were you before you were a gentleman?"

Wit, skilfully used, is the kindliest and most effective method of exhibiting the futility of judicial interruptions.

"Where do you draw the line, Mr. Bramwell?" asked a learned judge in the Court of Common Pleas.

"I don't know, and I don't care, my lord. It is enough for me that my client is on the right side of it."

Wit and courtesy need never be divorced. They are, indeed, complementary. Wit, deftly used, refreshes the spirit of the weary judge.

Lord Chief Justice Coleridge, writing from the Northern Circuit, says: "Gully was excellent. His phrase, when he asked for a stay of execution 'in order to consider more at leisure some of your lordship's observations,' tickled my fancy very much. Misdirection was never more courteously described."

Satire or irony is often in danger of being misunderstood by the simple-minded jury. Ridicule, to be effective, must be pointed, even extravagant.

In combating the defence of Act of God set up by an American advocate defending a client on the charge of arson, Governor Wisher, for the prosecution, disposed of the theory of spontaneous combustion, and succeeded in satisfying the jury of its absurdity: "It is said, gentlemen, that this was Act of God. It may be, gentlemen. I believe in the Almighty's power to do it, but I never knew of His walking twice round a straw stack to find a dry place to fire it, with double-nailed boots on so exactly fitting the ones worn by the defendant."

Bowen, on the Western Circuit, was less fortunate. Prosecuting a burglar caught red-handed on the roof of a house, he left the case to the jury in the following terms: "If you consider, gentlemen, that the accused was on the roof of the house for the purpose of enjoying the midnight breeze, and, by pure accident, happened to have about him the necessary tools of a housebreaker, with no dishonest intention of employing them, you will, of course, acquit him." The simple sons of Wessex nodded complacently at counsel, and, accepting his invitation, acquitted the prisoner.

And as there is danger of satire being misunderstood, there is also a certain danger that an advocate, in an endeavour to shorten a case, may fail to drive home all the points he seeks to make. Modern advocates, however, are more likely to remind the Bench of Quintilian's maxim, "There is not so much inconvenience in listening to superfluous matter as to be ignorant of such things as are necessary," than to remember the more pertinent first principle of their own art that "brevity is the soul of wit."

It has always been a reproach to our advocacy that it injured its clients by calculated circumlocution, an exuberance of verbosity, and a prolixity of style and method ruinous to the widows and the fatherless and the strangers that strayed within the gates of the temple.

Good advocacy displays the highest form of wit in an instinct for brevity. The healthy appetite of judge and advocate alike is shown in a keenness to "get through the rind of the orange and reach the pulp as soon as possible." This wit and wisdom of Bramwell should be painted on the wall in bold letters of silver opposite every judge on the bench, and in larger letters of gold over every bench in the kingdom in the face of the nation's advocates.

Judges are, indeed, a long-suffering race, but there are some advocates difficult to suffer gladly. Mr. Justice Wightman showed a Christian forbearance to Mr. Ribton, who, after pounding away for several hours, began repeating himself unto the third or fourth iteration.

"Really, Mr. Ribton, you know, you've said that before."

"Have I, my lord? I am very sorry. I quite forgot it."

"Don't apologise," said the mild old judge, patiently stifling a sigh. "I forgive you; for it was a very long time ago."

How many advocates weary juries into forgetfulness by long-continued repetition of their cross-examination, often giving a clever witness opportunities of rehabilitating himself, forgetting Josh Billings's immortal advice: "When you strike ile, stop boring; many a man has bored clean thru and let the ile run out of the bottom."

But whatever sound maxims may be cited, it is to be feared that there will always be a line of advocacy answering to the definition of length without breadth. Nor will the old story, first told, perhaps, of Chief Baron Kelly, ever want a new and even more long-winded hero. A legal comrade of Kelly on circuit dreamed that they appeared before the tribunal on the Great Day of Judgment. Upon Kelly's name being called, and his being put up in the dock, the recording angel arose and shouted out in a loud voice, "No other case will be taken to-day!"

Lest I should provoke a similar reproof from a devout reader, let me leave the Lamp of Wit upon the altar of justice and retire from the pulpit.

V

THE LAMP OF ELOQUENCE

V

THE LAMP OF ELOQUENCE

THE eloquence of advocates of the past must largely be taken on trust. There is no evidence of it that is not hearsay. For, though we have the accounts of ear-witnesses of the eloquence of Erskine, Scarlett, Choate, or Lincoln, and can ourselves read their speeches, the effect of their eloquence does not remain. We are told about it by those who experienced it, and can believe or not as we choose. It is the same with actors. It requires genius to describe acting, so that the reader captures some of the experience of the witness. Fielding did it for Garrick when he took Partridge to see *Hamlet*; Charles Lamb can feature the old actors for us on the screen of the written page; but how few real records remain of the eloquence of the advocates of old!

Perhaps the best way to realise their powers is to read their speeches aloud; but even then they seem diffuse and out of proportion to the present interest in the litigation. The most eloquent advocacy that is reported in print is to be found not in law reports, but in fiction—in the speeches of Portia and Serjeant Buzfuz, for instance, where for all time the world continues hanging on the lips of the advocate in excited sympathy with the client.

There are some who think that rhetoric at the Bar has fallen in esteem. The modern world has certainly lost its taste for sweet and honeyed sentences, and sets a truer value on fine phrases and the fopperies of the tongue; but there will always be a high place in the profession for the man who speaks good English with smooth elocution, and whose speeches fall within Pope's description:

> Fit words attended on his weighty sense,
> And mild persuasion flow'd in eloquence.

The test of eloquence in advocacy is necessarily its effect upon those to whom it is addressed. The aim of eloquence is persuasion. The one absolute essential is sincerity, or, perhaps one should say, the appearance of sincerity. As Garrick reminded a clerical friend: "We actors portray fiction as if it were truth, and you clergymen preach truth as if it were fiction." It is no use preaching to a jury, but the eloquence of persuasion will work miracles; and there is a well-authenticated story on every circuit of the criminal who, listening with rapt attention to his counsel's pathetic details of his wrongs, burst into sobs after his peroration, crying out, "I never knew I was such an ill-used man until now—s'help me, I never did!"

It would appear from the history of advocacy that the flame of the lamp of eloquence may vary from time to time in heat and colour. One cannot say that the style of one advocate is correct and another incorrect, since the style is the attribute of the man and the generation he is trying to persuade. Yet, however different the style may be, the essential power of persuasion must be present. He must, as Hamlet says, be able to play upon his jury, knowing the stops, and sounding them from the lowest note to the top of the compass.

Brougham's tribute to Erskine's eloquence is perhaps the best pen-picture of an English advocate we possess, and it is noticeable how he emphasises this power of persuasion and endeavours to solve the psychology of it. He places in the foreground the physical appearance of the man, a great factor in each style of advocacy.

"Nor let it be deemed trivial," he says,

"or beneath the historian's province, to mark that noble figure, every look of whose countenance is expressive, every motion of whose form graceful, an eye that sparkles and pierces, and almost assures victory, while it 'speaks audience ere the tongue.' Juries have declared that they felt it impossible to remove their looks from him when he had riveted and, as it were, fascinated them by his first glance; and it used to be a common remark among men who observed his motions that they resembled those of a blood-horse, as light, as limber, as much betokening strength and speed, as free from all gross superfluity or encumbrance. Then hear his voice of surpassing sweetness, clear, flexible, strong, exquisitely fitted to strains of serious earnestness, deficient in compass indeed, and much less fitted to express indignation, or even scorn, than pathos, but wholly free from harshness or monotony. All these, however, and even his chaste, dignified, and appropriate action, were very small parts of this wonderful advocate's excellence. He had a thorough knowledge of men, of their passions, and their feelings—he knew every avenue to the heart, and could at will make all its chords vibrate to his touch. His fancy, though never playful in public, where he had his whole faculties under the most severe control, was lively and brilliant; when he gave it vent and scope it was eminently sportive, but while representing his client it was wholly subservient to that in which his whole soul was wrapped up, and to which each faculty of body and of mind was subdued—the success of the cause."

And if one reads the speeches of our greatest advocates and the records of those who heard them, one finds that each had some peculiar condiment of eloquence, so that if one could beg a flavour from each one might hope to produce an olio of super-eloquence.

Bethell, for instance, was a master of deliberation, remembering Bacon's maxim that "a slow speech confirmeth the memory, addeth a conceit of wisdom to the hearers." Shorthand-writers listened eagerly to his speeches, fearing to miss a sentence that would ruin their report. Repetitions and unnecessary phrases were banned, and useless words he looked upon as matter in the wrong place. His voice was clear and musical, and he had a telling wit. Students from the first thronged the court to learn his magic, and judges listened to him with respect. When he was a junior it is said that Sir John Leach, the Master of the Rolls, succumbing to his arguments, said, "Mr. B*ee*thell, you understand the matter as you understand everything else." And that was the real secret of Mr. Bethell's eloquence.

Serjeant Copley, better known as Lord Lyndhurst, was not a brilliant or showy advocate, but, as a friend said, "had no rubbish in his head." He won many of his triumphs by dexterous and successful sophistry and his extreme plausibility of manner. Mr. James Grant tells us that "a perpetual smile played on his countenance while he gazed at the faces of the court and the jury; and there was something so winning in the tones of his voice that he must have been a man possessing a remarkably lively perception of the real facts of a case, of a vigorous intellect, and of great energy of character who was not carried away by Mr. Copley's address." The mere wording of the description might suggest to an unsympathetic reader that Serjeant Copley was the Fascination Fledgeby of the Bar, but the intention of the writer was probably to portray something of that charm of manner which is often a form of eloquence leading to the highest success in advocacy. Gully, in our own day, possessed it in a high degree. It is easy to fall under the spell of it in court, but it would require the pen of a genius to recall it to life on the printed page.

Eloquence of manner is real eloquence, and is a gift not to be despised. There is a physical as well as a psychological side to advocacy, documentary evidence of which may be found in the old prints and portraits of those who have been called to high office from among us. They are, on the whole, a stout, well-favoured race.

Charm of voice and manner has always received due reward. Thomas Denman had a fine, musical voice, an easy manner, and the sincerity and fervour of his address made him a popular advocate. Scarlett was "the very incarnation of contentedness and good nature." A spectator notes his "perpetual cheerfulness," his "laughing and seductive eyes," his "How-do-you-do style" as he used to stand before the jury, "fold up the sides of his gown on his hands, and then, placing his arms on his breast, smile in their faces from the beginning to the end of his address, talking all the while to them as if he were engaged on a mere matter of friendly conversation."

Many an advocate has attempted a similar method with but small success, and there must have been, as Mr. Atlay says, "an exquisite dexterity" in his method of address that does not reach us through contemporary descriptions. The effect of it was undoubted. A North-Country juryman was once asked, after a long assize at Lancaster, "What do you think of the counsellors on the Northern Circuit?"

"Why," he replied, "there's not a man in England can touch that Mr. Brougham."

"But you gave all the verdicts to Mr. Scarlett?"

"Why, of course; he gets all the easy cases."

It is eloquence that persuades the jury that your case is the easy case. As Cobbett said—and Cobbett had a common jury mind—"He is an orator that can make me think as he thinks, and feel as he feels."

Mr. Montagu Williams has pointed out that the best English eloquence of his time was founded on what he calls a solid style of advocacy. "As leading examples," he writes, "of what I may call the solid style, I should name Serjeant Shee, Serjeant Parry, and Lord Justice Holker. When I say 'solid,' I do not refer to heaviness of manner, but to solidity of appearance, robustness of speech, and a general air of good English honesty. This style is very taking with the juries of this country. It was the heavy, nay, almost languid, way in which Lord Justice Holker opened his cases, taken in conjunction with his sudden awakenings and bursts of eloquence when important points were reached, that rendered his style of advocacy so telling."

Nearly every great advocate has found it necessary to make use of the eloquence of persuasion. Charles Russell is the one exception. He did not seek to persuade, he directed the court and jury. Whether or not he was, as Lord Coleridge said, "the biggest advocate of the century," he was undoubtedly a very great advocate. Clearness, force, and earnestness were the basic qualities of his eloquence. It was said of him that "ordinarily the judge dominates the jury, the counsel, the public, —he is the central figure of the piece. But when Russell is there the judge isn't in it. Russell dominates every one."

But no man can dominate a jury in a doubtful case, and though Russell was supreme in a good case, he had not that power possessed in a high degree by another great advocate—still, happily, among us—Sir Edward Clarke, who could not only insinuate doubts into the hearts of the jury, but could leave his arguments so clearly in men's minds that he became, as it were, the thirteenth man on the jury when they retired to consider their verdict. This requires real eloquence.

The moral of the lives of the advocates seems to be that in the house of eloquence there are many mansions, and any style natural to the man who uses it is his right style, and may succeed. One besetting sin of many would-be eloquent speakers is fatal, and that is bombast. The young advocate who opened a libel case, "My client, gentlemen, is a cheesemonger; and the reputation of a cheesemonger is like the bloom upon a peach. Touch it, and it is gone for ever," must have been immune from eloquence. Yet there are solicitors and clients who still like that kind of thing, and advocates who supply it.

Nearer to eloquence was the advocate who, in defence of a woman for child murder, said in passionate tones: "Gentlemen, it is impossible that the prisoner can have committed this crime. A mother guilty of such conduct to her own child! Why, it is repugnant to our better feelings! Gentlemen, the beasts of the field, the birds of the air, suckle their young——"

The simile might perhaps have passed with the jury had not a dry, unsympathetic voice from the bench interrupted with : " Mr. X, if you establish the latter part of your proposition, your client will be acquitted to a certainty."

And though eloquence at its highest is a gift, the art of speaking can be learned and personal difficulties overcome. Demosthenes, with his pebbles in his mouth or running up a hill spouting an oration, has been an example to us from the schoolroom. Cicero took lessons from Roscius and Æsop. Lord Guildford, Lord Campbell, Lord Brougham, and others have impressed on students the importance of attending and practising at moots and debating societies. The mechanics of eloquence can be as certainly learned by the student as the mechanics of etching or engraving, but how far these will make an artist of him and help to bring real eloquence to the learner lies in himself.

There is no golden rule of method, but there is this golden principle to remember that the message of eloquence is addressed to the heart rather than the brain. This is well put by Lord Chesterfield, who was more human than many will allow, when he wrote to his son : " Gain the heart, or you gain nothing ; the eyes and the ears are the only road to the heart. Merit and knowledge will not gain hearts, though they will secure them when gained. Pray have that truth ever in your mind. Engage the eyes by your address, air, and motions; soothe the ears by the elegancy and harmony of your diction; the heart will certainly follow; and the whole man and woman will as certainly follow the heart."

Thus is the grammar of the matter set down by a skilled grammarian, yet it is but a bundle of dry sticks and kindles no flame. The high privilege of lighting the torch at the lamp of eloquence is a gift of the gods, for orators are born, and not made.

VI

THE LAMP OF JUDGMENT

VI

THE LAMP OF JUDGMENT

Judgment inspires a man to translate good sense into right action. I would not quarrel with the philosopher who describes judgment as an instinct, but I would bid him remember that even an instinct is acquired by "cunning" rather than luck. Let no one think that he can attain to sound judgment without hard work. The judgment of the advocate must be based on the maxim, "He that judges without informing himself to the utmost that he is capable cannot acquit himself of judging amiss."

A client is entitled to the independent judgment of the advocate. Whether his judgment is right or wrong, it is the duty of the advocate to place it at the disposal of his client. In the business of advocacy judgment is the goods that the advocate is bound to deliver. Yet he is under constant temptation to please his client by giving him an inferior article. The duty of the advocate to give only his best is wisely insisted upon by Serjeant Ballantine, who relates a personal experience that all advocates must be ready to face.

"The solicitor instructing me," he writes, "was vehement in expressing belief in his client's innocence. I was of a different opinion. He, acting upon his belief, desired that certain witnesses should be called. I, governed by my convictions, absolutely refused to do so, offering at the same time to return my brief. This, however, was refused, and I was left to exercise my own responsibility. The above question frequently arises, and some counsel have considered themselves bound to obey the wishes of the solicitor. There is no doubt that this is the safest course for the advocate, for, if he does otherwise and the result is adverse, he is likely to be much blamed, and the solicitor also is exposed to disagreeable comments; but I hold, and have always acted upon the opinion, that the client retains counsel's judgment, which he has no right to yield to the wishes or opinions of any one else. He is bound, if required, to return his brief, but if he acts against his own convictions he sacrifices, I think, his duty as an advocate."

An advocate of judgment has the power of gathering up the scattered threads of facts and weaving them into a pattern surrounding and emphasising the central point of the case. In every case there is one commanding theory, to the proof of which all the facts must be skilfully marshalled. An advocate with one point has infinitely greater chances than an advocate with twenty points.

Rufus Choate was an advocate of great judgment, and not only was he enthusiastic and diligent in searching for the central theory, or "hub of his case," as he called it, but having made up his mind what it was, he rightly put it forward without delay, believing that it was the "first strike" that conquered the jury. Parker, his biographer, tells us that "he often said to me that the first moments were the great moments for the advocate. Then, said he, the attention is all on the alert, the ears are quicker, the mind receptive. People think they ought to go on gently, till, somewhere about the middle of their talk, they will put forth all their power. But this is a sad mistake. At the beginning the jury are all eager to know what you are going to say, what the strength of your case is. They don't go into details and follow you critically all along: they try to get hold of your leading notion, and lump it all up. At the outset, then, you want to strike into their minds what they want—a good, solid, general view of *your* case; and let them think over that for a good while. 'If,' said he emphatically, 'you haven't got hold of them, got their convictions at least open, in your first half-hour or hour, you will never get at them at all.'"

Abraham Lincoln had a genius for seeing the real point of his case and putting it straight to the Court. A contemporary who was asked in later life what was Lincoln's trick with the jury replied, "He saw the kernel of every case at the outset, never lost sight of it, and never let it escape the jury. That was the only trick I ever saw him play."

Sir Henry Hawkins held the same view. He used to say, "Concentration is the art of argument. If you are diffuse, you will be cut up in detail." And he was fond of quoting the teachings of Denman on this subject: "Remember also to put forward your best points first, for the weak ones are very likely to prejudice the good ones if they take the lead. It would be better advice to say never bring them forward at all, because they are useless."

Johnny Williams, who appeared with Brougham and Denman for Queen Caroline, was a man of great sagacity, but much given to strong expletives. He was once induced by an attorney, against his own better judgment, to ask a question, the answer to which convicted his client on a capital charge. The circuit considered he was well justified, when the trial was over, in turning to the attorney and saying with great emphasis (formal expletives omitted), " Go home, cut your throat, and *when* you meet your client in hell, beg his pardon."

But an apology was also due from Williams for surrendering his judgment to that of his attorney.

In nothing does the advocate more openly exhibit want of judgment than in prolixity. Modern courts of justice are blamed by the public, not wholly without cause, for the length and consequent expense of trials. To poor people this may mean a denial of justice. No one desires that the judge should constantly interfere with counsel in the discharge of their duties, but it seems to be his duty on occasion to blow his whistle and point out to the combatants that they are offside.

If every one connected with the trial of an action were to train and use his judgment and co-operate with the judgments of his fellow-workers in a policy of anti-waste, a great reproach would be lifted from our courts of justice.

Prolixity is no new disease. Many wise judges have sought to eradicate it. In the time of Charles II. things seem to have been in a specially bad way, and Lord Guildford, though he probably went to dangerous extremes, was well thought of by the public for his endeavour to speed up the legal machine.

"In his lordship's conduct of trials he was very careful of three matters: 1. To adjust what was properly the question, and to hold the counsel to that; for he that has the worst end of the staff, is very apt to fling off from the point and go out of the right way of the cause. 2. To keep the counsel in order; for in trials they have their parts and their times. His lordship used frequently to inculcate to counsel the decorum of evidencing practice. 3. To keep down repetition, to which the counsel, one after another, are very propense; and, in speeching to the jury one and the same matter over and over again, the waste of time would be so great that, if the judge gave way to it, there would scarce be an end; for most of the talk was not so much for the causes as for their own sakes, to get credit in the country for notable talkers. And his lordship often told them that their confused harangues disturbed the order of his thoughts ; and, after the trial was over, it was very hard for him to resume his method and direct the jury to comprise all the material parts of the evidence. Therefore he was positive not to permit more than one counsel of a side to speech it to the jury, by way of summing up the evidence ; and he permitted that in such a way as made them weary of it. For, in divers sorts of trials, he wholly retrenched it ; and where he observed much stiffness and zeal of the parties in a cause, then, after the evidence was over, he would say, 'Come, make your speeches ; ' and then sat him down : and that looked with a sort of contempt of their talents, which gave them a distrust, and discomposed their extempore so much that, for the most part, they said, 'No, we will leave it to your lordship.' And thus the abuse, by fastidious talk, wore away ; and the practice before him was so well known, as it became at length a pure management of evidence and argument of law."

The judgment of an advocate may be called upon at any moment for a sudden decision that may mean the victory or defeat of his client. For this reason it is necessary that he should be always alert. The contents of his brief must be already in his mind, and his attention must be fixed on what is happening in court, which has rarely been foreseen in the best-prepared brief ever delivered to counsel.

It was Russell who turned round to his junior and said, "What are you doing?"

"Taking a note," was the answer.

At which Russell burst out in his uncompromising way: "What the devil do you mean by saying you are taking a note? Why don't you watch the case?"

"Watch the case!" It is a golden rule.

It was the same when he was playing cards. He would get impatient with a partner shuffling and handling his cards in a state of indecision. "Why are you looking at your cards?" he asked. "Why don't you watch the game? The game is on the table."

In the same way an advocate who is always fumbling with his brief when he is examining a witness cannot follow the game that is on the table before him.

Sound judgment is essential to the examination of witnesses. How few advocates know how to examine a witness-in-chief! Birrell tells us that Sir Frank Lockwood had very clear views on the subject. "He believed that the examination of a witness-in-chief, or the direct examination of witnesses, as it was called in Ireland, was very much underrated in its significance and its importance. If they had to examine a witness, what they had got to do was to induce him to tell his story in the most dramatic fashion, without exaggeration; they had got to get him, not to make a mere parrot-like repetition of the proof, but to tell his own story as though he were telling it for the first time—not as though it were words learnt by heart; but if it were a plaintive story, plaintively telling it. And they had got to assist him in the difficult work. They had got to attract him to the performance of his duty, but woe be to them if they suggested to him the terms in which it was to be put! They must avoid any suspicion of leading the witness, while all the time they were doing it. They knew perfectly well the story he was going to tell; but they destroyed absolutely the effect if every minute they were looking down at the paper on which his proof was written. It should appear to be a kind of spontaneous conversation between the counsel on the one hand and the witnesses on the other, the witness telling artlessly his simple tale, and the counsel almost appalled to hear of the iniquity under which his client had suffered.

"It was in this way, and in this way

alone, that they could effectively examine a witness."

There is probably more waste of time and irrelevance in the examination of witnesses-in-chief than in any other procedure of counsel. This is the modern drama of it.

COUNSEL (*his eyes glued to his brief*): "Your name is Mary Ann Snooks."

WITNESS (*annoyed*): "Martha Ann."

COUNSEL: "Oh, yes, Martha Ann Snooks; and you are the wife of Thomas Snooks, the bookmaker."

WITNESS (*very indignant*): "Nothing of the sort."

COUNSEL: "I beg your pardon—my mistake—bootmaker."

WITNESS: "And has been this thirty year——"

COUNSEL: "And you live at 139 Doncaster Street, Upper Tulse Hill."

WITNESS: "We did live there; we've moved now, sir."

COUNSEL: "What is your present address?"

etc., etc., *ad lib*.

Consider for a moment, if you will, the horrid waste of all this irrelevance standing between the Court and Mrs. Snooks's version of what she saw of an accident in High Street, Kensington, and reducing her to a state of nervous irritation antipathetic to accurate testimony.

How much more business-like was the method of the eighteenth century! In a State trial in the days of Queen Anne the name of the lady is announced in the oath, and then counsel approaches her, as Sir Frank Lockwood might have done: "Pray, madam, will you be pleased to acquaint my lord and the jury what you know concerning the matter, and what passed between your brother Mr. Colepepper and Mr. Denew at his first coming to him?"

Much public time could be saved by more economical methods of examination-in-chief, and greater efficiency would be ensured.

Cross-examination, too, is almost entirely a matter of judgment. Two golden rules handed down from the eighteenth century, and maybe from beyond, are still unlearned lessons to each succeeding generation of advocates:

1. Never ask a question without having a good reason to assign for asking it.

2. Never hazard a critical question without having good ground to believe that the answer will be in your favour.

Serjeant Ballantine has some just observations on the art of cross-examination and the use and abuse of it.

"The records of justice," he says, "from all time show that truth cannot, in a great number of cases tried, be reasonably expected. Even when witnesses are honest, and have no intention to deceive, there is a natural tendency to exaggerate the facts favourable to the cause for which they are appearing, and to ignore the opposite circumstances; and the only means known to English law by which testimony can be sifted is cross-examination. By this agent, if skilfully used, falsehood ought to be exposed, and exaggerated statements reduced to their true dimensions. An unskilful use of it, on the contrary, has a tendency to uphold rather than destroy. If the principles upon which cross-examination ought to be founded are not understood and acted upon, it is worse than useless, and it becomes an instrument against its employer. The reckless asking of a number of questions on the chance of getting at something is too often a plan adopted by unskilful advocates, and noise is mistaken for energy. Mr. Baron Alderson once remarked to a counsel of this type, 'Mr. ——, you seem to think that the art of cross-examination is to examine crossly.'"

How few advocates have the capacity to let well alone! They must repeat and emphasise, and emphasise and repeat. In a case tried before Sir Henry Hawkins, a junior, not content with his own witness's answer, continues :

JUNIOR (*emphatically*): "And you are quite sure of this ?"

WITNESS : "Yes."

JUNIOR : "Quite ?"

WITNESS : "Quite !"

JUNIOR : "You have no doubt about it ?"

WITNESS : "Well, I haven't much doubt, because I asked my wife."

SIR HENRY (*pouncing on his prey*): "You asked your wife in order to be sure in your own mind ?"

WITNESS : "Quite so, my lord."

SIR HENRY : "Then you had some doubt before ?"

WITNESS : "Well, I may have had, my lord."

It is part of the advocate's rôle to make the jury believe in his infallibility, and every question he asks that gives the witness an opportunity to score off him and belittle him in their eyes is an error of judgment. Serjeant Buzfuz, who conducted his case with fine judgment, was guilty of a grave error in his examination of Sam Weller. Brow-beating is always a dangerous policy ; it antagonises the jury and leads to reprisals. There is an old story of the counsel in an assault case who asked the witness at what distance from the parties he was at the time of the assault. Not content with the reply of "A few feet," but pressing for greater accuracy, he was answered by the witness: "Just four feet five and a half inches."

"How do you come to be so very exact, fellow?" asked counsel sternly.

"Because I expected some fool or other would ask me, so I measured it."

A good story, too, is told against Lord Coleridge in Mr. O'Brien's *Life of Lord Russell*. He appeared in a libel action for a young lady who had been expelled from a college. His case was that the breaches of discipline were trivial, and he pressed Mrs. Kennedy, the mistress of novices, asking what his young client had done. Mrs. Kennedy said, as an example, that she had eaten strawberries.

"Eaten strawberries!" exclaimed Coleridge. "What harm was there in that?"

"It was forbidden, sir," replied Mrs. Kennedy simply.

Coleridge should have accepted her answer, but he retorted with a contemptuous question, not foreseeing the reprisal, "But, Mrs. Kennedy, what trouble was likely to come from eating strawberries?"

"Well, sir," replied Mrs. Kennedy, "you might ask what trouble was likely to come from eating an apple, yet we know what trouble did come from it."

Coleridge's cross-examination dissolved in laughter, in which, of course, he joined good-naturedly.

The art of re-examination, which is a task often as futile as the endeavour to set Humpty Dumpty on the wall again, can be learned only by the experience of watching the game on the table and playing any few remaining cards in your hand with rapid judgment.

A wise student will take Lord Halsbury's advice and go to the Old Bailey to study cross-examination; and, if Lockwood's view still holds good, he might attend the Chancery Courts to learn how not to re-examine. Birrell tells us that "once, in the Court of Chancery, a witness was asked, in cross-examination by an eminent Chancery leader, whether it was true that he had been convicted of perjury. The witness owned the soft impeachment, and the cross-examining counsel very promptly sat down. Then it became the duty of an equally eminent Chancery Q.C. to re-examine. 'Yes,' said he, 'it is true you have been convicted of perjury. But tell me, have you not on many other occasions been accused of perjury, and been acquitted ? ' "

Most re-examination intending to rehabilitate the character of a witness is apt to make matters worse.

These stories of actual happenings, trivial in themselves, teach us the necessity of judgment in advocacy. And I pray the young advocate not to rejoice too merrily over the errors of judgment of his seniors or lament too grievously about his own. Bear in mind that by acknowledged error we may learn wisdom, and that the only illuminant for the lamp of judgment is the oil of experience.

VII

THE LAMP OF FELLOWSHIP

VII

THE LAMP OF FELLOWSHIP

An advocate lacking in fellowship, careless of the sacred traditions of brotherhood which have kept the lamp of fellowship burning brightly for the English Bar through many centuries, a man who joins the Bar merely as a trade or business, and does not understand that it is also a professional community with public ideals, misses the heart of the thing, and he and his clients will suffer accordingly.

Fitzjames Stephen wisely said of the English Bar that it is "exactly like a great public school, the boys of which have grown older, and have exchanged boyish for manly objects. There is just the same rough familiarity, the general ardour of character, the same kind of unwritten code of morals and manners, the same kind of public opinion expressed in exactly the same blunt, unmistakable manner."

The very title of Inns of Court is redolent of hospitality, fellowship, and even conviviality. How many glorious things have their beginnings at an inn! How pleasant it would be to investigate with the antiquarians the earliest origins of our Inns of Court! But to come to comparatively modern days, Sir John Fortescue, who was Chief Justice of the King's Bench in the time of Henry VI., gives us a pleasant picture of their traditions of fellowship. These Inns of Court, or hostels, he says, anciently received the sons of noble men and the better sort of gentlemen, "who did there not only study the laws to serve the courts of justice and profit their country, but did further learn to dance, to sing, to play on instruments on the ferial days and to study divinity on the festival, using such exercises as they did who were brought up in the King's Court." There were Inns of Chancery, too, where the younger students learned the first elements of law before they were taken into the greater hostels, which were called Inns of Court. The expenses of the student were no less than twenty marks a year in Fortescue's day, and if he was attended by his servant, as most were, that was an added charge, so that only the sons of gentlemen could afford so expensive an education.

At this time a young fellow would come

from the university, or perhaps straight from the grammar-school, and would learn the first elements of law in one of the ten minor Inns of Chancery, and would then apply for admission to one of the four houses or Inns of Court : Inner or Middle Temple, Gray's Inn or Lincoln's Inn. There they continued for the space of seven years, attending readings, moots—where cases were put and discussed—and "boltings," as the practice arguments were called, "whereby," as Fortescue tells us, "growing ripe in the knowledge of the laws, and approved withal to be of honest conversation, they are either by the general consent of the benchers or readers (being of the most ancient, grave, and judicial men of every Inn of Court), or by the special privilege of the present reader there, selected and called to the degree of utter (outer) barristers, and so enabled to be common counsellers and to practise the law both in their chambers and at the bars."

The whole social scheme of education and control in the exercise of professional rights and advancement was most carefully thought out. An utter barrister of not less than ten or twelve years' standing and "of good profit in study" was chosen as reader to educate the students. At about fifteen years' standing he became a bencher, after which he might be appointed a serjeant, and go away to Serjeants' Inn, that important society "where none but serjeants and judges do converse," and from which alone could judges be chosen.

It was for this reason that the judges always addressed a serjeant as "Brother." I can well remember as a boy feeling a certain glow of satisfaction at hearing the judges in the Tichborne trial calling my father "Brother Parry," and it seems a pity that this fraternal greeting, this courteous link of fellowship between Bench and Bar, necessarily disappeared with the abolition of Serjeant's Inn. Yet, though the talisman is no longer spoken, the spirit of brotherhood will always be with us.

In the old days education in the law was undertaken very seriously, but in a fraternal spirit. The reader would propound a case, the utter barristers would declare their opinion, the reader would confute the objections laid against him, and the students would eagerly note the learned points of the seniors. These readings took four or five hours daily, and were held in the halls. The moots and the boltings took place after supper, and at other times among the students under the leadership of a barrister.

But the whole term was not taken up with the dry study of the law. There were feastings, grand nights, and, greatest of all, the Christmas Saturnalia, at one of which, after a costly dinner, a pack of hounds was brought into the hall, a fox and a cat were let loose, and a mad hunt took place. Isaac D'Israeli gives an excellent account of these wild doings, taken from a rare tract supposed to have been written in 1594. "Supper ended," he writes, "the constable-marshal presented himself, with drums playing, mounted on a stage borne by four men, and carried round; at length he cries out, 'A lord, a lord,' &c., and then calls his mock court every one by name.

"'Sir Francis Flatterer, of Fowlshurt.

"'Sir Randall Rackabite, of Rascal-hall, in the county of Rake-hell.

"'Sir Morgan Mumchance, of Much Monkery, in the county of Mad Mopery.

"'Sir Bartholomew Bald-breech, of Buttock-bury, in the county of Break-neck.'

"They had also their mock arraignments. The king's-serjeant, after dinner or supper, 'oratour-like,' complained that the constable-marshal had suffered great disorders to prevail; the complaint was answered by the common-serjeant, who was to show his talent at defending the cause. The king's-serjeant replies; they rejoin, &c.: till one at length is committed to the Tower, for being found most deficient. If any offender contrived to escape from the lieutenant of the Tower into the buttery, and brought into the hall a manchet (or small loaf) upon the point of a knife, he was pardoned; for the buttery in this jovial season was considered as a sanctuary. Then began the *revels*. Blount derives this term from the French *reveiller*, to awake from sleep. These were sports of dancing, masking comedies, &c. (for some were called solemn revels), used in great houses, and were so denominated because they were performed by night; and these various pastimes were regulated by a master of the revels.

"Amidst 'the grand Christmass' a personage of no small importance was 'the Lord of Misrule.' His lordship was abroad early in the morning, and if he lacked any of his officers, he entered their chambers to drag forth the loiterers; but after breakfast his lordship's power ended, and it was in suspense till night, when his personal presence was paramount, or, as

Dugdale expresses it, 'and then his power is most potent.'

"Such were then the pastimes of the whole learned bench; and when once it happened that the under-barristers did not dance on Candlemas Day, according to the ancient order of the society, when the judges were present, the whole bar was offended, and at Lincoln's Inn were by decimation put out of commons, for example-sake; and should the same omission be repeated, they were to be fined or disbarred; for these dancings were thought necessary, 'as much conducing to the making of gentlemen more fit for their books at other times.'"

The details of the alliteration with which Sir Francis Flatterer and others are called into court have always interested me deeply, as on the Northern Circuit, when the crier at Grand Court calls in the absent ones, he has to do it in curious and measured phrases of alliterative abuse. When Fitzjames Stephen was made crier on account of his stentorian voice, his delicate mind revolted against the coarseness of his duties, and he sought to have the Circuit Court and its ancient, outspoken manners abolished, but fortunately he did not succeed.

For though some of this ancientry is

better honoured in the breach than the observance, yet even the buffoonery, as Stephen called it, of Grand Court has its value as a link with the past.

It is an excellent thing for the profession that in the same way as the lessons of advocacy in the past were learned by the young students from their elders, who sat at meat with them and shared their lives in intimate and homely fashion, so to-day we enter a common Inn, dine at a common table, join a common mess upon circuit, all of which is evidence of the continuance of that right spirit of fellowship which, to my mind, is an essential of advocacy.

The fellowship of the Temple springs from its long traditions of brotherhood among the Templars. To turn out of the Strand into its quiet courts brings over your brooding spirit something of that sacred melancholy pleasure which one feels on entering the old school or dining once again in the college hall. But you are no longer actor, art and part, in the school and college life. Here in the Temple, though others are judges and benchers and fashionable leaders, you can still wander in shabby honesty in the gardens, pull down some of the old volumes in the library, and dine below the salt with your fellow-ancients.

Thackeray has a true insight into the pleasures of memory that the Temple possesses for those who have lived there, and pictures, as he alone can, its historic charm.

"Nevertheless," he writes, "those venerable Inns which have the Lamb and Flag and the Winged Horse for their ensigns have attractions for persons who inhabit them, and a share of rough comforts and freedom which men always remember with pleasure. I don't know whether the student of law permits himself the refreshment of enthusiasm, or indulges in poetical reminiscences as he passes by historical chambers and says, 'Yonder Eldon lived—upon this site Coke mused upon Lyttelton—here Chitty toiled—here Barnwell and Alderson joined in their famous labours—here Byles composed his great work upon bills, and Smith compiled his immortal leading cases—here Gustavus still toils, with Solomon to aid him:' but the man of letters can't but love the place which has been inhabited by so many of his brethren, or peopled by their creations, as real to us at this day as the authors whose children they were—and Sir Roger de Coverley, walking in the Temple Garden and discoursing with Mr. Spectator about the beauties in hoops and patches who are sauntering over the grass, is just as lovely a figure to me as old Samuel Johnson rolling through the fog with the Scotch gentleman at his heels on their way to Dr. Goldsmith's chambers in Brick Court; or Harry Fielding, with inked ruffles and a wet towel round his head, dashing off articles at midnight for the *Covent Garden Journal* while the printer's boy is asleep in the passage."

The Temple is full of ghosts—honest ghosts with whom it is a privilege to claim fellowship.

There are some who speak of the Bar sneeringly as a Trade Union—which it certainly is, and to my thinking one of the oldest and best unions. And if advocacy could be honestly described as a trade, then the phrase trade union might be accepted without demurrer. For the basic quality of a trade union, that which has made these institutions thrive against opposition, is the spirit of fellowship and unselfishness which is the ideal of its members.

We have seen how of old the senior members of the Bar trained up the juniors in the mystery of their craft, and throughout the practice of the profession it has always been a point of honour for the elders to assist the beginners in those difficult days of apprenticeship.

What could be more delightful and encouraging to a youngster than to be received by his genial, handsome leader in the presence of an admiring attorney after the fashion that Montagu Williams tells us of his first meeting with Serjeant Shee? "I shall never forget," he writes, "my consultation with dear old Serjeant Shee. I knew very little about pleadings, and matters of that kind, and so the work naturally made me feel somewhat nervous. On going upstairs to the consulting-room to see Serjeant Shee, whom I already knew slightly, I had my briefs stuck under my arm, somewhat ostentatiously, I am afraid. The old serjeant patted me on the shoulder and said, 'Lots of briefs flowing in, my boy; delighted to see it.'

"When we had taken our seats, and the consultation had begun, he said, turning to the solicitor who instructed us, 'Winning case—pleadings all wrong. That young dog over there smelt it out long ago, as a terrier would a rat, I can see—eh, Montagu Williams? You've found it out; I can see it by your face.'

"Heaven knows I was as innocent of finding anything out as the man in the moon. I sniggered feebly; and then the serjeant proceeded to put into my mouth the vital blots in the case of our adversary, which he alone had discovered.

" That was the way leaders treated their juniors then. I must leave my successors at the Bar to decide whether or not things are the same now."

With equal kindness that great man and honest advocate, Abraham Lincoln, stretched out the hand of welcome and encouragement to the younger men who came along.

James Haines tells us the story of his first brief, The People *v.* Gideon Hawley. " There were," he says, " thirty-two indictments against my client for obstructing a public road, and as the authorities were inclined to make an example, the case was somewhat serious. I retained Mr. L. to conduct the defence, and after we had completed our preparations he said, ' Of course, you will make the opening speech.' I was surprised, for I had supposed that he would want to assume full control, and I said as much, adding that I would prefer him to take the lead. ' No,' he answered, and then, laying a hand on my shoulder, he continued : ' I want you to open the case, and when you are doing it, talk to the jury as though your client's fate depends on every word you utter. Forget that you have any one to fall back upon, and you will do justice to yourself and your client.' I have never forgotten the kind, gentle, and tactful manner in which he spoke those words," Mr. Haines continued, "and that is a fair sample of the way he treated the younger members of the Bar."

No man ever attains a position at the Bar in which he can afford to despise the opinion of his fellow-men. The eulogies of public journals, even the praise and patronage of attorneys, are of no worth compared with the respect of the Bar. As a French advocate wrote: "A solid reputation proceeds only from the Court."

Charles Russell, who stood on a somewhat lonely eminence at the head of his profession, and dealt with the affairs of his fellows in a very rough-handed and independent manner, was at heart very jealous of the good opinion of the Bar.

He had, during the course of a trial, cross-examined a lady with great severity, and afterwards received an anonymous letter of a very abusive character, in which he was charged with having been guilty of conduct in his cross-examination "which no gentleman should pursue towards any woman." He thereupon sat down and wrote a letter to the counsel on the other side, in which he said, "I should be sorry to think this was true, but I am not the best judge of my own conduct," and asked for his learned friend's opinion on the charge.

The interesting point of the correspondence is that Russell felt that it might possibly be true. It reminds one of the celebrated line in a lively mid-Victorian comedy, where the servant-girl said, "Really, ma'am, I'm that flustered that I don't know whether I am standing on my head or my heels." To which Mrs. John Wood used to reply with stern emphasis, "No decent woman ought to have the slightest doubt on a subject of that kind."

Russell's learned friend cleverly evaded responsibility by telling him that the character of a gentleman was one "we all know you eminently possess," with which certificate of character the great man was soothed and satisfied.

With the decay of circuits and the passing of old customs and the silence of ancient convivialities, some of the spirit of fellowship may be lost. But we must remember that even the good old days were not without evidence of professional malice and uncharitableness. As far back as the reign of François I. it was a rule of the French Bar that "advocates must not use contentious words or exclamations the one toward the other; or talk several at the same time, or interrupt each other." These words might still be engraved in letters of gold on the walls of our own law-courts, for on occasion the lamp of fellowship burns so low that such things occur. Still, at the English Bar we may claim that we set a good example to other bodies of learned men by our real attachment to the precepts and practice of fellowship, and may, without hypocrisy, commend the rest of mankind to follow in our footsteps,

> And do as adversaries do in law,
> Strive mightily, but eat and drink as friends.

For it is by keeping the lamp of fellowship burning that we encourage each other to walk in the light of the seven lamps of advocacy.

INDEX